WORLD CUP 2010

AN UNAUTHORIZED GUIDE

Michael Hurley

Raintree

www.raintreepublishers.co.uk
Visit our website to find out more information about Raintree books.

To order:
☎ Phone 0845 6044371
🖷 Fax +44 (0) 1865 312263
✉ Email myorders@capstonepub.co.uk

Customers from outside the UK please telephone +44 1865 312262

Raintree is an imprint of Capstone Global Library Limited, a company incorporated in England and Wales having its registered office at 7 Pilgrim Street, London, EC4V 6LB – Registered company number: 6695582

Text © Capstone Global Library Limited 2010
First published in hardback in 2010
Paperback edition first published in 2010
The moral rights of the proprietor have been asserted.

Edited by Louise Galpine and Vaarunika Dharmapala
Designed by Steve Mead and Ken Vail Graphic Design
Picture research by Hannah Taylor
Originated by Capstone Global Library Ltd
Printed and bound in China by CTPS

ISBN 978 0 431044 35 4 (hardback)
14 13 12 11 10
10 9 8 7 6 5 4 3 2 1

ISBN 978 0 431044 40 8 (paperback)
14 13 12 11 10
10 9 8 7 6 5 4 3 2 1

British Library Cataloguing in Publication Data
Hurley, Michael
World Cup 2010. -- (The World Cup)
796.3'34668-dc22
A full catalogue record for this book is available from the British Library.

Acknowledgements
We would like to thank the following for permission to reproduce photographs: Corbis pp. **8** (Reuters/Jorge Silva), **10** (Christian Liewig), **12** (Liewig Media Sports/ Neil Marchand), **14** (epa/Fernando Bizerra JR), **18** (AMA/Matthew Ashton), **25** (Reuters/Siphiwe Sibeko); Corbis Saba p. **7** (Louise Gubb); Getty Images pp. **4** (Gallo Images/Lefty Shivambu), **9** (Ross Kinnaird), **11** (Jasper Juinen), **13** (Clive Brunskill), **19** (AFP/Daniel Garcia), **21** (AFP/Ian Kington); © KPT Power Photos background images; Press Association Images pp. **17** (AP Photo/Olivier Asselin), **20** (AP Photo/Lorenzo Galassi); Rex Features pp. **5** (Action Press), **16** (Giuliano Bevilacqua); Shutterstock background images (© Nikola I).

Cover photograph of Italian players lifting the World Cup trophy after winning the final against France in 2006, reproduced with permission of Corbis (epa/Daniel Dal Zennaro).

Every effort has been made to contact copyright holders of material reproduced in this book. Any omissions will be rectified in subsequent printings if notice is given to the publishers.

Disclaimer
All the Internet addresses (URLs) given in this book were valid at the time of going to press. However, due to the dynamic nature of the Internet, some addresses may have changed, or sites may have changed or ceased to exist since publication. While the author and publishers regret any inconvenience this may cause readers, no responsibility for any such changes can be accepted by either the author or the publishers.

CONTENTS

Some words are shown in the text in bold, **like this**.
You can find out what they mean by looking in the
glossary on page 31.

WORLD CUP 2010

The 2010 **FIFA** World Cup will be held in South Africa. Teams from 32 countries around the world will take part. The **tournament** kicks off on 11 June and the final will be played in Johannesburg on 11 July. It will be the first time that a World Cup is held on the African **continent**. South Africa is the only country that did not have to qualify for the tournament, because it will be the **host** nation.

The thirty-two teams will be placed into eight groups of four (see pages 28–29). Each team plays three group matches, gaining three points for a win, one point for a draw, and no points for losing. The two teams from each group with the most points will go through to a second round. The tournament then becomes a **knockout** competition.

Official mascot

Zakumi the leopard is the official mascot of the World Cup in South Africa. Whenever you see Zakumi, he has a football with him. He wants to encourage children to play football. Zakumi is a symbol of South Africa and the continent of Africa. He represents self-confidence, pride, hospitality, social skills, and warm-heartedness.

World Cup history

The first ever World Cup was played in Uruguay, in South America, in 1930. Uruguay won the tournament. There has been a World Cup every four years since then, except in 1942 and 1946 (because of World War II, 1939–1945). Italy won the last World Cup, held in Germany in 2006. Italy have won the trophy four times. Brazil is the most successful team in World Cup history. They have won the tournament five times.

Brazil's Ronaldo lifts the trophy as his team celebrates winning the World Cup final against Germany in 2002.

SOUTH AFRICA – THE HOST NATION

South Africa was chosen by **FIFA** to **host** the 2010 World Cup. The first professional **league** in the country was set up in 1959. Between 1964 and 1992, FIFA banned South Africa from taking part in FIFA **tournaments**. This was because of its system of government, called **apartheid**. In 1992, the ban was dropped and South Africa were allowed to play again.

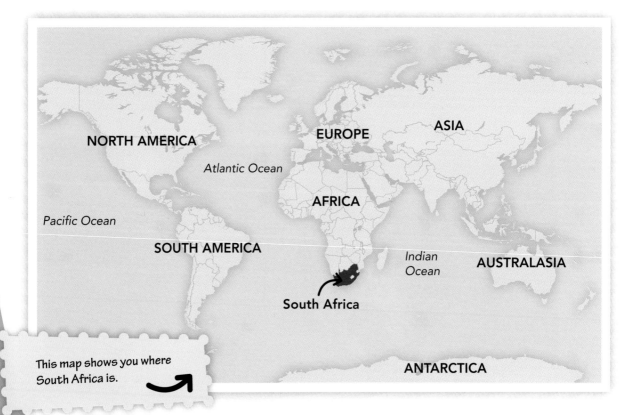

NORTH AMERICA

Atlantic Ocean

Pacific Ocean

SOUTH AMERICA

EUROPE

ASIA

AFRICA

Indian Ocean

AUSTRALASIA

South Africa

ANTARCTICA

This map shows you where South Africa is.

Apartheid

In 1950 the South African government set up laws for a system called apartheid. This system meant that people were treated differently depending on the colour of their skin. Black Africans had very few rights under apartheid. They were forced to live in areas away from white people. They were not allowed to share buses, trains, restaurants, cinemas, or hotels with white people. Many **activists** fought this racist system, but it stayed in place until 1991.

Nelson Mandela

Nelson Mandela is the most famous South African in history. In the 1960s, he was arrested and sent to Robben Island Prison for fighting against apartheid. He spent nearly 27 years in jail. In 1990 he was released and helped unite the country after years of unrest. In 1994 he became the first **democratically** elected president of South Africa.

Mandela is a great **ambassador** for South Africa and also does a lot of fundraising for charity. He has set up two foundations: the Nelson Mandela Foundation and the Nelson Mandela Children's Fund.

Nelson Mandela is respected and loved in South Africa and all around the world.

Famous footballer

Lucas Radebe made 70 appearances for South Africa before retiring in 2005. He was an excellent **defender**. In 1994 he transferred to Leeds United, in England, and became their captain in the late 1990s. The Leeds United fans loved Radebe's hard work and **influence** on the pitch. They nicknamed him "The Chief". Since he retired, he has been honoured by FIFA with a Fair Play Award for his work with children and against racism in football. He is an official FIFA ambassador.

Bafana Bafana

South-African football fans call their team *Bafana Bafana*. This means "the boys".

TEAMS TO WATCH

There will be 32 teams at the 2010 **FIFA** World Cup in South Africa. Countries from Europe, Africa, Asia, North America, and South America will be represented at the finals. Here are some of the favourites, potential winners, and teams with a chance of causing some shock results:

 ## Argentina

Argentina will be one of the favourites to win the 2010 World Cup. They have qualified for every World Cup since 1974 and have won the trophy twice. Their **strikers**, Sergio Aguero, Carlos Tevez, and Lionel Messi can cause problems for any opposition team.

STATS

WORLD CUP APPEARANCES: 14

WORLD CUP WINS: 2 (1978, 1986)

Carlos Tevez (middle) in action against Mexico during the Copa America tournament in 2007.

Brazil

Brazil are always thought of as one of the favourites to win the World Cup. They are the most successful team in the history of the **tournament**, with five wins. Brazil teams have had some of the greatest footballers ever, including Pelé, Garrincha, Zico, and Ronaldo. The current team includes Robinho, Kaka, Luis Fabiano, and Alexandre Pato. If these four exciting players can play well together, Brazil have an excellent chance of winning their sixth World Cup.

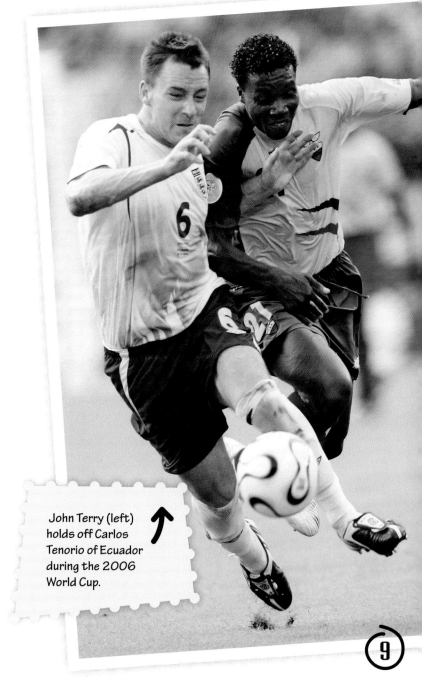

John Terry (left) holds off Carlos Tenorio of Ecuador during the 2006 World Cup.

STATS

WORLD CUP APPEARANCES: 18

WORLD CUP WINS: 5 (1958, 1962, 1970, 1994, 2002)

 England

England have won the World Cup only once, in 1966, but they are always expected to perform well at the tournament. They qualified for the World Cup after winning 9 out of 10 qualifying matches, scoring 34 goals, and only **conceding** 6. England have a strong and reliable defence, a hard-working midfield, and strikers with **pace**. Captain John Terry and his defensive partner Rio Ferdinand will need to be at their best.

STATS

WORLD CUP APPEARANCES: 12

WORLD CUP WINS: 1 (1966)

 France

France have some exciting players, such as Thierry Henry and Franck Ribery. They had a difficult qualifying campaign, but they still have the ability to cause any team problems during the **tournament**. France made it to the final of the 2006 World Cup, but lost to Italy.

Thierry Henry (right) is one of the most famous players on the France team. He has helped them gain two important victories, at the World Cup in 1998 and at the European Championships in 2000.

Germany

Germany **hosted** the last World Cup, in 2006. They played better than expected and reached the semi-finals. They have a solid team with a couple of outstanding players. Their captain Michael Ballack is a very talented **midfielder**. Striker Miroslav Klose has scored 10 goals in 14 World Cup appearances.

 ## *Italy*

Italy, the current holders of the World Cup, will be one of the favourites to win in 2010. In the 2006 final, they won on **penalties** against France. Many of the players from the 2006 **squad** will be available to play in South Africa. The experience of players such as Andrea Pirlo will be important for Italy if they are to repeat the success of 2006.

 ## *Spain*

Spain have the experience of winning the **UEFA** European Championships in 2008 and will be another favourite to win in 2010. The team play attractive passing football. Their **strikers** Fernando Torres and David Villa both have explosive **pace** and score lots of goals. Many people feel that Spain's goalkeeper, Iker Casillas, is the best in the world. He makes some amazing saves.

David Villa runs with the ball during a 2010 World Cup qualifying match. Villa was injured during the 2008 European Championships, so he will be hoping to play as many matches as possible at the World Cup.

USA

This is the ninth time the USA have qualified for the World Cup. They reached the quarter-finals in 2002 and will be trying to repeat this success in South Africa. Michael Bradley, who is the coach's son, could be a star for the USA at the World Cup this time.

STATS

WORLD CUP
APPEARANCES: 8

WORLD CUP WINS: 0

South Africa

South Africa will **host** the World Cup for the first time in 2010. The players will hope that the fans can help them to make it past the group stage of the **tournament** for the first time. Benni McCarthy and Steven Pienaar are South Africa's most famous players. They both also play in the English Premier **League**.

STATS

WORLD CUP
APPEARANCES: 2

WORLD CUP WINS: 0

Cameroon

Cameroon first played at a World Cup in 1982. They burst on to the world football scene by beating Argentina in the opening match of the 1990 World Cup. They went on to reach the quarter-finals that year. Since then, they have regularly qualified for the World Cup. Samuel Eto'o is Cameroon's most recognizable footballer.

STATS

WORLD CUP
APPEARANCES: 5

WORLD CUP WINS: 0

Samuel Eto'o (left) and Angola's Antonio Lebo-Lebo fight for the ball in the 2006 African Nations Cup.

 ## *Australia*

Australia will be appearing in their third World Cup. Australia had a good tournament in 2006, where they reached the second round. They were knocked out by a last-minute goal from Italy. Tim Cahill is one of Australia's most popular footballers and also plays in the English Premier League.

South Korean players celebrate winning a group stage match against Poland in the 2002 World Cup.

South Korea

South Korea have played in the last six World Cups. They co-hosted the tournament with Japan in 2002. South Korea reached the semi-final that year, and this was their most successful tournament. In Germany in 2006, South Korea were knocked out in the group stage. In South Africa, Ji-Sung Park (who also plays for Manchester United) will be appearing in his third World Cup.

PLAYERS TO WATCH

The 2010 **FIFA** World Cup will be an opportunity for some of the world's most outstanding footballers to show off their abilities. Here are some great players to watch out for:

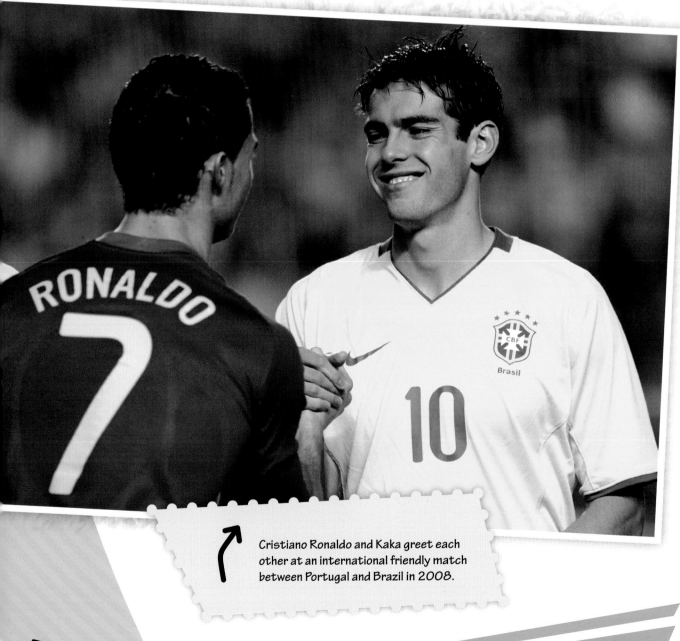

Cristiano Ronaldo and Kaka greet each other at an international friendly match between Portugal and Brazil in 2008.

Kaka (Brazil)

Kaka is the latest in a long line of Brazilian players with great **technique** and ball control. He can play as an attacking **midfielder** or as a **forward**. Kaka moved to Real Madrid in 2009. Before that, he won lots of trophies in his club career with AC Milan, including the **UEFA** Champions **League** in 2007. Kaka was named FIFA World Player of the Year in 2007.

WORLD CUP GAMES: 6
WORLD CUP GOALS: 1

 Cristiano Ronaldo (Portugal)

Cristiano Ronaldo is one of the most famous and recognizable footballers in the world. The Portuguese **winger** has amazing ball control and **dribbling** ability. Ronaldo is Portugal's most important player. He is skilful and has very good balance. He was named FIFA World Player of the Year in 2008, after he scored 42 goals in one season for his former club, Manchester United. Ronaldo moved to Real Madrid in 2009.

WORLD CUP GAMES: 6
WORLD CUP GOALS: 1

Wayne Rooney (England)

Wayne Rooney made his England **debut** in 2003 when he was only 17 years old. He has now played more than 50 times for England. Rooney is probably the best English footballer for over 20 years. He is fearless, strong, and has a very powerful shot.

WORLD CUP GAMES: 4
WORLD CUP GOALS: 0

Michael Essien (Ghana)

Michael Essien is a very hard-working midfielder. He is strong, athletic, and determined. Ghana made their World Cup debut in Germany, in 2006, and Essien was their outstanding performer.

WORLD CUP GAMES: 3
WORLD CUP GOALS: 0

Fernando Torres (centre) scores the winning goal against Germany in the 2008 **UEFA** European Championship final.

![Spain flag] **Fernando Torres**
(Spain)

Fernando Torres is one of the best **strikers** in world football. He is quick, strong, and can score with both his left and right foot, as well as with his head. He is a very important player for Spain.

WORLD CUP GAMES: 3
WORLD CUP GOALS: 0

Lionel Messi
(Argentina)

Lionel Messi is one of the most amazing talents in world football. He is a very quick player with tremendous **dribbling** ability. He can score and create goals. Many fans have compared Messi with former Argentina player Diego Maradona, who was captain of Argentina when they won the 1986 World Cup.

WORLD CUP GAMES: 3
WORLD CUP GOALS: 1

Didier Drogba celebrates during an African Nations Cup match against Ghana in 2008.

Didier Drogba
(Ivory Coast)

Ivory Coast striker Didier Drogba is one of the most recognizable footballers in the world. In 2006 he was named African Footballer of the Year. Drogba is tall, athletic, quick, and strong. He can cause problems for any **defender** in the world because of his determination and scoring ability.

WORLD CUP GAMES: 2
WORLD CUP GOALS: 1

YOUNG PLAYERS TO WATCH

Some players will be making their World Cup **debut** in 2010. These young players will have to deal with the pressure of performing at the World Cup for the first time. Here are a few to watch out for:

Theo Walcott
(England)

Theo Walcott was part of the England **squad** for the 2006 World Cup in Germany. He was only 17 and did not get an opportunity to play. Walcott has since become a very important member of the England team. His **pace** and goal-scoring could be vital for England at the 2010 World Cup.

Karim Benzema
(France)

Karim Benzema is a quick **striker** who will be very important for France if they hope to win the World Cup. Benzema is tall, athletic, and can score great goals with his powerful shots.

Theo Walcott just about to score a goal against Croatia in a 2010 World Cup qualifying match held in Zagreb, Croatia, in 2008. He scored an amazing hat-trick in this game.

Giuseppe Rossi
(Italy)

Giuseppe Rossi is an exciting **forward** who scores goals with his powerful shots. He is quick and skilful and could be important for Italy as they try to retain the World Cup. Rossi was born in the USA, but moved to Italy when he was 13 years old.

Alexandre Pato
(Brazil)

Brazil striker Alexandre Pato is a player with lots of skill. He is quick and has excellent ball control. He signed for AC Milan in 2007 when he was only 18 years old. He is now an important part of their team. He is also starting to become an important player for Brazil.

Sergio Aguero
(Argentina)

Sergio Aguero is one of Argentina's best players and one of the best young players in the world. He is a very skilful striker who scores lots of goals.

Sergio Aguero (right) in action for Argentina in a World Cup 2010 qualifying match. Argentina fans will be hoping that he can score lots of goals at the World Cup.

Marcello Lippi (Italy)

Marcello Lippi has been the manager of Italy twice. He was the manager when they won the **FIFA** World Cup in Germany in 2006, and returned to help Italy qualify for the 2010 World Cup.

During his managerial career Lippi has won many trophies. In Italy, he led Juventus to Italian **League** and **UEFA** Champions League success in the 1990s.

Marcello Lippi (centre) on the training pitch with his players in 2009.

Repeat success?

Marcello Lippi is not the only manager at the 2010 World Cup to have won the tournament before. Carlos Alberta Parreira, who is now the manager of South Africa, won the World Cup with Brazil in 1994.

Dunga (Brazil)

Dunga played in midfield for Brazil at three World Cups. He was Brazil's captain when they won the World Cup in 1994, in the USA. Dunga took over as Brazil manager after they were knocked out of the 2006 World Cup. He was an **inspirational** player and was a popular choice when he became the manager of Brazil.

The Brazil fans' expectations are very high because Brazil have won more World Cups than any other team. There is also pressure on the manager for Brazil to play attractive, attacking football.

Fabio Capello (England)

Fabio Capello is Italian but took over as England manager in December 2007.

Capello is one of the most successful club managers in world football. He has won the Italian League title with three different teams (AC Milan, Juventus, and Roma). His AC Milan team won the UEFA European Cup (now the Champions League) in 1994. He has also managed Real Madrid twice, winning the Spanish League title in 1997 and 2007.

Fabio Capello on the touchline during an England friendly match against Slovakia in 2009.

The hardest job in football?

The England manager's job is often said to be "the hardest job in world football" because the fans are so desperate for success. The manager and players are always under pressure to win. England manager Fabio Capello is one of the highest paid football managers in the world. He reportedly earns £6 million a year.

CITIES AND STADIUMS

Nine cities in South Africa will **host** matches at the 2010 **FIFA** World Cup. Ten different stadiums will be used. Johannesburg, the city with the highest population in South Africa, has two stadiums. Here is some information about the different cities and stadiums:

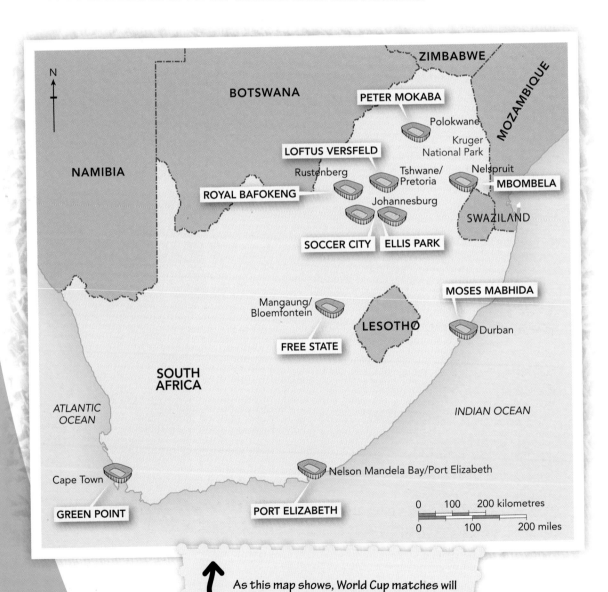

As this map shows, World Cup matches will be held all over South Africa.

Cape Town ▶

Cape Town is located on the south-west coast. It is a beautiful city with golden beaches and the world famous Table Mountain. Table Mountain is more than 1,000 metres (3,200 feet) high and has an unusual flat top.

Green Point Stadium

Green Point Stadium is one of five new stadiums that have been built for the 2010 World Cup. It is a world-class stadium that can be used for many different sports. The stadium is named after Green Point, an area of Cape Town. It will be used for one of the semi-finals.

BUILT: 2009 • **CAPACITY:** 70,000

Moses Mabhida Stadium

This new, three-tier stadium has a capacity of 70,000. Two large archways, each 100 metres (330 feet) high, curve over the stadium. It will be used for one of the World Cup semi-finals.

BUILT: 2009 • **CAPACITY:** 70,000

◀ Durban

Durban is on the south coast of South Africa. More than 3.3 million people live in Durban, making it the second biggest city in South Africa. It is the busiest port in Africa.

Free State Stadium

This stadium has been upgraded recently to increase capacity for the World Cup. A second tier has been added to the west side of the stadium.

BUILT: 1952 • **CAPACITY:** 48,700

Mangaung/ Bloemfontein ▶

Located right in the middle of the country, Mangaung/Bloemfontein is the capital of Free State province.

Port Elizabeth Stadium

This is a new stadium built for the 2010 World Cup.

BUILT: 2009 • **CAPACITY:** 48,000

◀ Nelson Mandela Bay/ Port Elizabeth

The first British settlers arrived in South Africa at Port Elizabeth in 1820. It is a busy port city on the south coast with a population of more than 1 million people. In 2000, Port Elizabeth became part of Nelson Mandela Bay, named after the former president of South Africa.

Nelspruit ▶

Located in the north-east of the country, Nelspruit is very close to a number of national parks including the world-famous Kruger National Park.

Mbombela Stadium

Until this stadium was built for the 2010 World Cup there was no world-class football stadium in this part of South Africa.

BUILT: 2009 • **CAPACITY:** 46,000

Peter Mokaba Stadium

This new stadium, built for the 2010 World Cup, is named after Peter Mokaba. He was born in Polokwane and worked as a political **activist** during the years of **apartheid**.

BUILT: 1999 • **CAPACITY:** 42,000

◀ Polokwane

Polokwane is a small city in the far north-east with a population of more than half a million people. Polokwane translates as "place of safety".

Royal Bafokeng Stadium

The Royal Bafokeng Stadium is named after the Bafokeng people who live in the area. The stadium was built in 1999 and upgraded for the 2010 World Cup.

BUILT: 1999 • **CAPACITY:** 42,000

Rustenburg ▶

Rustenburg is in the north. Named by Dutch settlers in 1851, Rustenburg means "place of rest" in Dutch.

Loftus Versfeld Stadium

One of the oldest stadiums in South Africa, Loftus Versfeld has been used for many international football matches. A recent upgrade increased the capacity to 50,000.

BUILT: 1909 • **CAPACITY:** 50,000

◀ Tshwane/Pretoria

Pretoria is part of Tshwane, a region established in 2000 that includes 13 separate areas. Tshwane has a population of more than 2 million people.

Johannesburg ▼

Johannesburg, or Jo'burg as the locals call it, is the largest city in South Africa. It is located in the north of the country and has a population of more than 3.6 million people.

Local derby

The Soweto derby, named after an area of Johannesburg, is played between two local teams, Kaizer Chiefs and Orlando Pirates.

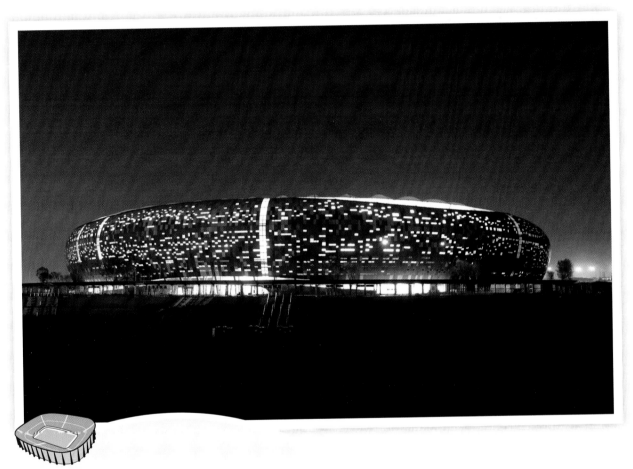

Soccer City Stadium

South Africa built its first football-only stadium in 1987. Soccer City Stadium has three tiers. The capacity has been raised by almost 15,000, to 94,700 for the World Cup. The first and last matches of the 2010 World Cup will be played here.

BUILT: 1987 • **CAPACITY:** 94,700

Ellis Park

Ellis Park is one of South Africa's oldest and most famous stadiums. It was originally built in 1928, but was rebuilt in the 1980s.

BUILT: 1928 • **CAPACITY:** 62,000

WORLD CUP 2010 TEAMS

Nation	Previous World Cup appearances	Best finish in a World Cup	Star player
Algeria	2	Group stage 1982, 1986	Nadir Belhadj
Argentina	14	Winners 1978, 1986	Lionel Messi (see pp. 8, 17)
Australia	2	Second round 2006	Tim Cahill (see p. 13)
Brazil	18	Winners 1958, 1962, 1970, 1994, 2002	Kaka (see pp. 9, 14, 15)
Cameroon	5	Quarter-final 1990	Samuel Eto'o (see p. 12)
Chile	7	Semi-final 1962	Alexis Sanchez
Denmark	3	Quarter-final 1998	Nicklas Bendtner
England	11	Winners 1966	Wayne Rooney (see p. 15)
France	12	Winners 1998	Franck Ribery (see p. 10)
Germany	18	Winners 1954, 1974, 1990	Miroslav Klose (see p. 10)
Ghana	1	Second round 2006	Michael Essien (see p. 15)
Greece	1	Group stage 1994	Theofanis Gekas
Honduras	1	Group stage 1982	Wilson Palacios
Italy	16	Winners 1934, 1938, 1982, 2006	Gianluigi Buffon
Ivory Coast	1	Group stage 2006	Didier Drogba (see p. 17)
Japan	3	Second round 2002	Shunsuke Nakamura

Nation	Previous World Cup appearances	Best finish in a World Cup	Star player
Mexico	13	Quarter-final 1986	Andres Guardado
Netherlands	8	Runners-up 1974, 1978	Robin van Persie
New Zealand	1	Group stage 1982	Ryan Nelsen
Nigeria	3	Second round 1994, 1998	Obafemi Martins
North Korea	1	Quarter-final 1966	Yong Jo Hong
Portugal	4	Semi-final 1966, 2006	Cristiano Ronaldo (see pp. 14, 15)
Paraguay	7	Second round 1986, 1998, 2002	Roque Santa Cruz
Serbia	0	–	Nemanja Vidic
Slovakia	0	–	Marek Hamsik
Slovenia	1	Group stage 2006	Milivoje Novakovic
South Africa	2	Group stage 1998, 2002	Steven Pienaar (see p. 12)
South Korea	7	Semi-final 2002	Ji-Sung Park (see p. 13)
Spain	8	Semi-final 1950	Fernando Torres (see pp. 11, 16)
Switzerland	8	Quarter-final 1934, 1938, 1954	Tranquillo Barnetta
Uruguay	10	Winners 1930, 1950	Diego Forlan
USA	8	Semi-final 1930	Michael Bradley (see p. 12)

WORLD CUP 2010 SCHEDULE

GROUP MATCHES

	Friday June 11	Saturday June 12	Sunday June 13	Monday June 14	Tuesday June 15	Wednesday June 16	Thursday June 17	Friday June 18	Saturday June 19	Sunday June 20	Monday June 21	Tuesday June 22	Wednesday June 23	Thursday June 24	Friday June 25
Johannesburg Soccer City	1 A1vA2			9 E1vE2			20 B1vB3			29 G1vG3			39 D1vD1		
Johannesburg Ellis Park		3 B1vB2			14 G1vG2			22 C4vC2			32 H1vH3			41 F4vF1	
Nelspruit Mbombela						15 H3vH4				28 F1vF3			40 D2vD3		46 G2vG3
Rustenburg Royal Bafokeng		5 C1vC2			12 F3vF4				24 D4vD2			33 A2vA3		43 E2vE3	
Mangaung/ Bloemfontein Free State				10 E3vE4			19 B4vB2			27 F4vF2		34 A4vA1			48 H2vH3
Cape Town Green Point	2 A3vA4			11 F1vF2				23 C1vC3		30 G4vG2				44 E4vE1	
Durban Moses Mabhida			7 D1vD2			16 H1vH2			25 E1vE3			35 B2vB3			45 G4vG1
Polokwane Peter Mokaba			6 C3vC4				18 A4vA2					36 B4vB1		42 F2vF3	
Nelson Mandela Bay/Port Elizabeth Port Elizabeth		4 B3vB4			15 G3vG4			21 D1vD3			31 H4vH2			37 C4vC1	
Tshwane/ Pretoria Loftus Versfeld			8 D3vD4			17 A1vA3			26 E4vE2				38 C2vC3		47 H4vH1

GROUP A		GROUP B		GROUP C		GROUP D	
1. South Africa	3. Uruguay	1. Argentina	3. South Korea	1. England	3. Algeria	1. Germany	3. Serbia
2. Mexico	4. France	2. Nigeria	4. Greece	2. USA	4. Slovenia	2. Australia	4. Ghana

ROUND OF 16						QUARTER-FINALS				SEMI-FINALS		3/4 PLACE AND FINAL	
Saturday June 26	Sunday June 27	Monday June 28	Tuesday June 29	Wednesday June 30	Thursday July 1	Friday July 2	Saturday July 3	Sunday July 4	Monday July 5	Tuesday July 6	Wednesday July 7	Thursday July 8 · Friday July 9	Saturday July 10	Sunday July 11

	52 1Bv2A (2)					58 1v3 (A)								64 Winner I v Winner II
		54 1Gv2H (7)					60 6v8 (D)							
50 1Cv2D (3)				Rest Days				Rest Days				Rest Days		
	51 1Dv2C (4)													
			56 1Hv2G (8)				59 2v4 (B)			61 AvC (I)				
		53 1Ev2F (5)									62 BvD (II)			
49 1Av2B (1)							57 5v7 (C)							
			55 1Fv2E (6)											63 Loser I v Loser II

GROUP E		GROUP F		GROUP G		GROUP H	
1. Netherlands	3. Japan	1. Italy	3. New Zealand	1. Brazil	3. Ivory Coast	1. Spain	3. Honduras
2. Denmark	4. Cameroon	2. Paraguay	4. Slovakia	2. North Korea	4. Portugal	2. Switzerland	4. Chile

FIND OUT MORE

Books to read

Essential Sports: Football (2nd edition), Andy Smith (Heinemann Library, 2008)

Football: The Ultimate Guide (Dorling Kindersley Publishers Ltd, 2008)

Sports Files: Wayne Rooney, John Townsend (Raintree, 2008)

The Usborne Little Book of Soccer Skills (Usborne Publishing Ltd, 2005)

Websites

www.fifa.com

This website has up-to-the-minute information about the FIFA World Cup, including photos and videos. You can also find statistics about all the players and countries who will be competing.

http://news.bbc.co.uk/sport1/hi/football

You can follow the World Cup, and see match results and reports as they happen on the BBC Sports news pages. This site is great for finding out how your favourite players and teams are performing.

GLOSSARY

activist person who fights for a cause

ambassador person who represents a country or raises awareness of an activity or issue

apartheid system that keeps people apart because of their skin colour

conceding allowing the other team to score against your team

continent one of the world's largest land masses, usually divided into many countries. There are seven continents on Earth.

debut first appearance. A footballer's first match is their debut.

defender position of a player on the pitch. Defenders try to stop the opposition from scoring.

democratically when everyone has the right to vote in an election

dribbling running with the ball

FIFA (*Fédération Internationale de Football Association*) international organization responsible for football around the world

forward position of a player on the pitch. Forwards can score goals or help other players to score.

host [*noun*] team or person that holds an event; [*verb*] act as host of an event

influence setting a good example that others want to follow

inspirational make people feel they can do something

knockout in a knockout competition, the winner of the match goes through to the next round and the loser is "knocked out" of the competition completely

league group of teams that compete against each other during the football season. There are national leagues all around the world.

midfielder player positioned in the middle of the field who helps the attacking and defending players

pace speed. A player who has lots of pace can move around the pitch very quickly.

penalties after extra time, if the scores are still level, the two teams pick five players from each team to try and score five penalties. The team that scores the most penalties wins.

squad group of players from which a team is chosen. A football squad is usually made up of around 20–23 players, from which a team of 11 is chosen.

striker position of a player on the pitch. Strikers try to score goals.

technique way of doing something. Different players control the ball in different ways on the football pitch, and there is good and bad technique for certain passes and skills.

tournament organized number of matches that lead to a final. The winner of the final game wins the tournament.

UEFA (Union of European Football Associations) organization responsible for European football

winger position of a player on the pitch. Wingers play on the outer edges of the pitch and usually try to create chances for their team to score.

INDEX